P9-AQN-745

Adventure
SPORTS

Rock
CLIMBING

Stephanie Turnbull

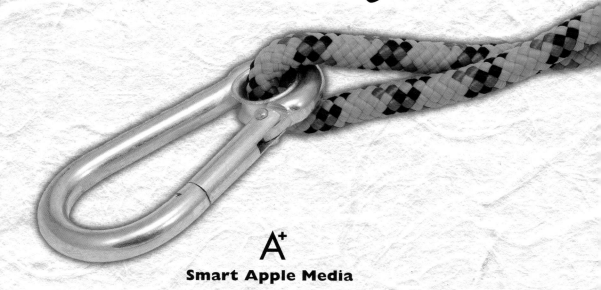

A+
Smart Apple Media

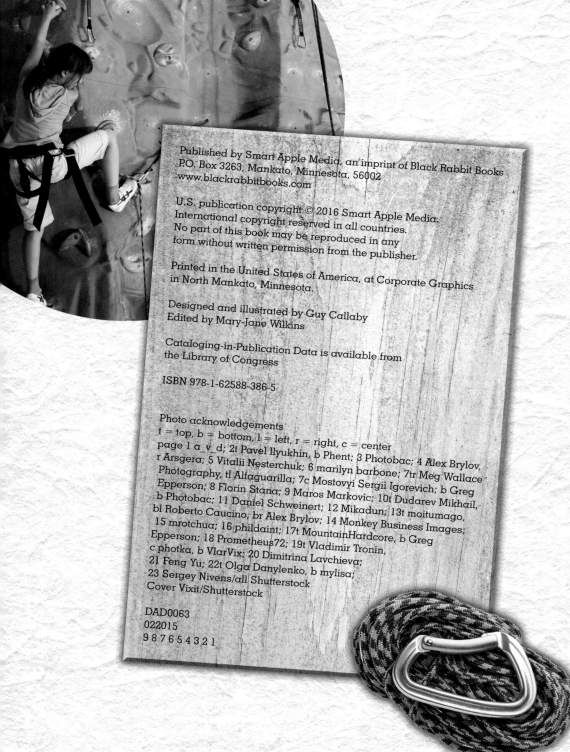

Published by Smart Apple Media, an imprint of Black Rabbit Books
P.O. Box 3263, Mankato, Minnesota, 56002
www.blackrabbitbooks.com

U.S. publication copyright © 2016 Smart Apple Media.
International copyright reserved in all countries.
No part of this book may be reproduced in any
form without written permission from the publisher.

Printed in the United States of America, at Corporate Graphics
in North Mankato, Minnesota.

Designed and illustrated by Guy Callaby
Edited by Mary-Jane Wilkins

Cataloging-in-Publication Data is available from
the Library of Congress

ISBN 978-1-62588-386-5

Photo acknowledgements
t = top, b = bottom, l = left, r = right, c = center
page 1 a_v_d; 2t Pavel Ilyukhin, b Phent; 3 Photobac; 4 Alex Brylov,
r Arsgera; 5 Vitalii Nesterchuk; 6 marilyn barbone; 7tr Meg Wallace
Photography, tl Alfaguarilla; 7c Mostovyi Sergii Igorevich; b Greg
Epperson; 8 Florin Stana; 9 Maros Markovic; 10t Dudarev Mikhail,
b Photobac; 11 Daniel Schweinert; 12 Mikadun; 13t moitumago,
bl Roberto Caucino, br Alex Brylov; 14 Monkey Business Images;
15 mrotchua; 16 phildaint; 17t MountainHardcore, b Greg
Epperson; 18 Prometheus72; 19t Vladimir Tronin,
c photka, b VlarVix; 20 Dimitrina Lavchieva;
21 Feng Yu; 22t Olga Danylenko, b mylisa;
23 Sergey Nivens/all Shutterstock
Cover Vixit/Shutterstock

DAD0063
022015
9 8 7 6 5 4 3 2 1

SEP 12 2016

CONTENTS

Feel the thrill   4

Get the gear   6

The right ropes   8

Tough training   10

Teamwork   12

Winter climbing   14

Stony scrambles   16

Smart planning   18

Emergency!   20

Glossary   22

Websites   23

Index   24

FEEL THE THRILL

Think you have the skill, strength, and stamina to give rock climbing a go? If you like exercise, excitement, and extreme heights, then read on...

Take the challenge

Imagine climbing a sheer rock face, inching upward with aching hands and gritted teeth, scrabbling for footholds in crumbling cracks. Imagine dangling over an **abyss**, moments from disaster, before hauling yourself onto a narrow ledge. Rock climbing tests you to the limit!

EXTREME BUT TRUE The world's highest mountain is Mount Everest, at 29,035 feet (8.848m). It's still being pushed up an inch or so every year—but it's also constantly worn away by **erosion**, so stays the same height.

There are places all over the world to try rock climbing, many with fantastic views.

Tough stuff

Don't even think of attempting rock climbing without the proper skills and knowledge—it's far too difficult and dangerous. You'll need to get fit, train hard, and find good teammates to climb with.

The more you practice, the more skilled you'll become at climbing even the steepest rock faces.

THRILL SEEKER

Adam Potter (Scotland)

FEAT
Survived a 984 foot (300 m) fall down mountain with only minor injuries

WHERE AND WHEN
Scotland, 2011

GET THE GEAR

Rock climbing gear is designed to keep you safe and help you tackle all kinds of climbs. Buy or hire the right stuff and learn how to use it.

Hats and harnesses

As well as ropes, you need a helmet and a comfortable harness. There are different harness types, including some with safety buckles, adjustable leg loops, a waist belt, and plenty of padding.

helmet

harness

Find a comfortable helmet and harness, and get used to wearing them. You'd be crazy to climb without them!

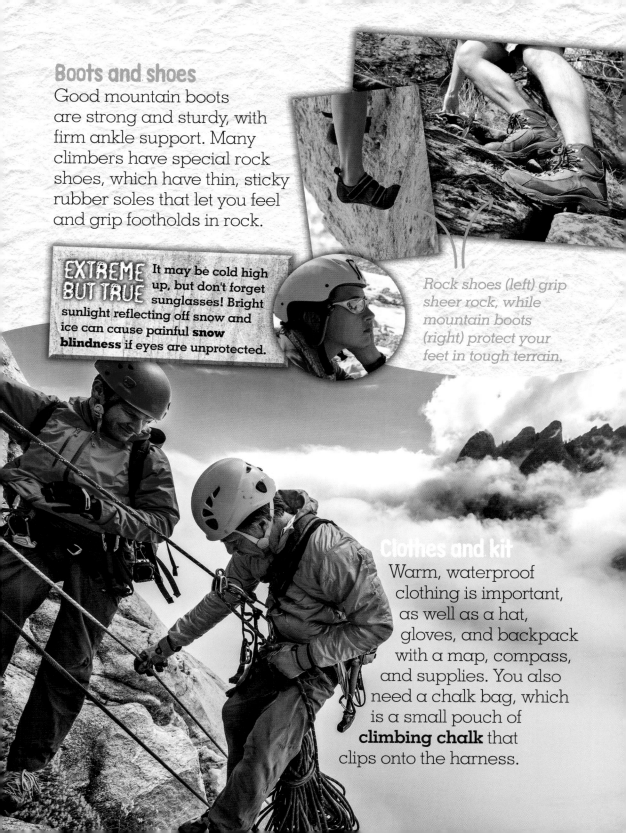

Boots and shoes

Good mountain boots are strong and sturdy, with firm ankle support. Many climbers have special rock shoes, which have thin, sticky rubber soles that let you feel and grip footholds in rock.

EXTREME BUT TRUE It may be cold high up, but don't forget sunglasses! Bright sunlight reflecting off snow and ice can cause painful **snow blindness** if eyes are unprotected.

Rock shoes (left) grip sheer rock, while mountain boots (right) protect your feet in tough terrain.

Clothes and kit

Warm, waterproof clothing is important, as well as a hat, gloves, and backpack with a map, compass, and supplies. You also need a chalk bag, which is a small pouch of **climbing chalk** that clips onto the harness.

THE RIGHT ROPES

Every rock climber needs good ropes. Climbing rope is smooth and very strong. It's also slightly stretchy, so if you fall it won't pull tight and jolt your body.

Rope stops you from falling far, and won't snap—it's strong enough to hold a two-ton truck!

Modern climbing rope has a thick elastic center and a tough outer layer.

Rope buddies

Most people climb in pairs so they're always attached by rope to another person, who holds the rope firm to steady them if they fall. This is called belaying. Read more about it on pages 12-13.

Get knotting

Knowing how to tie proper knots is vital. It means you can fix ropes securely to the rock face (using **anchors** attached to the rock) and to your harness—and untie them easily, too. Here are a few useful knots.

THRILL SEEKER

Colby Coombs (U.S.)

FEAT

Survived an **avalanche** thanks to his rope, which stopped him being swept away by falling snow

WHERE AND WHEN

Mount Foraker, Alaska, 1992

Figure of eight
Attaches rope to harness

Bowline
Makes a loop at end of rope

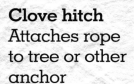

Clove hitch
Attaches rope to tree or other anchor

Overhand
Stops end of rope from unraveling

Slacklining is a sport in which people walk along a climbing rope tied between two trees. It takes amazing balance and lots of nerve, especially when done over dizzying drops in the mountains!

EXTREME BUT TRUE

TOUGH TRAINING

You don't need to be a muscle-bound giant to climb well. The keys are balance, confidence, and steady, controlled footwork that uses as little energy as possible.

Legs not arms

Legs and feet are stronger than arms, so first find a good foothold and step into it firmly. Shift your weight carefully over it before moving the second foot, so you don't lose balance. Now look for handholds and push up with your legs—don't pull with your arms or you'll soon be tired.

Use your legs to push yourself up while gripping useful handholds with your fingers.

Climbing walls

Indoor climbing walls are a great place to learn. Remember: it's better to make several small moves than huge steps that strain your body and leave you hot and exhausted. Stick to positions that feel comfortable.

EXTREME BUT TRUE Your brain prepares your body for exercise by pumping **adrenaline** into your bloodstream. This gives muscles a boost to help them work extra hard.

Choose footholds that are nearby and don't make you stretch awkwardly.

THRILL SEEKER

Edward Whymper (England)

FEAT

First person to reach Matterhorn **summit** (his ninth attempt)

WHERE AND WHEN

Alps, border of Italy and Switzerland, 1865

TEAMWORK

It's great to climb with other people. Friends keep you company, give you support when you're tired, and may save your life if you fall!

How to belay

If you're climbing with a friend, learn to belay (see page 8). For this you need a belay device.

rope attached to first climber

The first climber fixes a rope to their harness and passes it down to the other person, through anchors in the rock. The second climber threads the rope through the belay device and clips it to their harness using a ring called a **carabiner**.

belay device

other end hangs down

carabiner

harness

EXTREME BUT TRUE Climbers used to be tied together by rope connecting their waists. If one fell, the rope might hurt their chest and stop them breathing— and pull their friend off the rock too!

The belay device lets the second person give out or take in rope as the first person climbs ahead. If they slip or stumble, the lower climber can prevent them from falling by using the belay device to quickly stop the rope.

Climbing talk

Keep talking to your friend as you go. Climbers often use simple, set words that avoid confusion and are heard easily over other noises, such as roaring rivers or whistling wind.

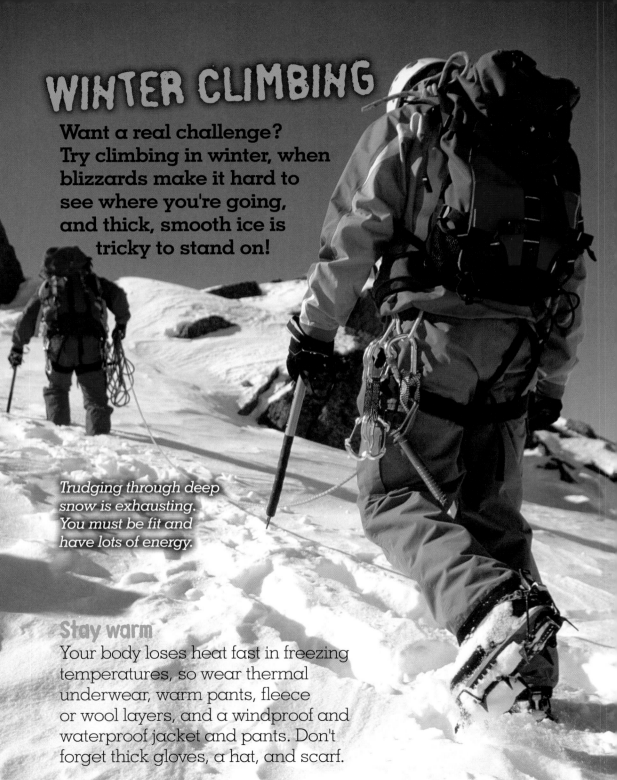

WINTER CLIMBING

Want a real challenge? Try climbing in winter, when blizzards make it hard to see where you're going, and thick, smooth ice is tricky to stand on!

Trudging through deep snow is exhausting. You must be fit and have lots of energy.

Stay warm

Your body loses heat fast in freezing temperatures, so wear thermal underwear, warm pants, fleece or wool layers, and a windproof and waterproof jacket and pants. Don't forget thick gloves, a hat, and scarf.

14

Ice gear

Two items you won't get far without are crampons, which go over your boots and help you grip ice, and an ice ax for hacking out hand and foot holds. Pack a backpack with survival gear (see pages 18-19)—you may need it!

Modern crampons and ice axes are made of strong but lightweight metal, so they're easy to carry.

air hole

Snow holes

Remember that snow can keep you warm if conditions are too bad to keep climbing. Dig into a deep drift with an ice ax or snow shovel. Make a hole big enough to sit in and cut blocks of snow to close the entrance.

Make an air hole and sit on your backpack or spare clothes to keep off the cold ground.

EXTREME BUT TRUE Frostbite is a painful condition that can affect exposed body parts such as your fingers and toes. They ache and throb, then become hard and waxy... and could even drop off if not treated!

STONY SCRAMBLES

Scrambling is a cross between rock climbing and a steep, tough hike. You need to use your hands and feet and be prepared to jump, slide, and slip around!

The toughest scrambling trails wind right to the top of mountains.

Rough rocks

Scrambling paths are steep climbs over exposed rocks, often with long drops below. You can usually manage them without ropes, but take care—crumbling rocks can be unstable, and wet or icy ground is slippery. Go with a friend and don't take risks.

THRILL SEEKER

Aron Ralston (U.S.)

FEAT

Survived 5 days trapped under a boulder that fell on his arm; escaped by hacking off his arm with a pocket knife

WHERE AND WHEN

Utah, 2003

Scramble skills

Use your basic climbing skills for scrambling. Move steadily, keep your weight over your feet for balance and push with your legs rather than pulling yourself up with your hands.

Scrambles can have very steep sections. Check the route before you set off.

EXTREME BUT TRUE A more extreme version of scrambling is rock hopping, where climbers take risky leaps from one rock to another, or even jump in and out of water.

SMART PLANNING

Adventure and excitement can easily become dangerous if you don't plan your trip well. Here are some hints to help you stay safe.

Know your limits

Routes are graded according to difficulty, so choose one at the right level for you. Always travel with a friend, let other people know where you're going, and stick to the path. Never be afraid to turn back if the going gets too tough.

EXTREME BUT TRUE **GPS receivers** use signals from satellites to tell you where you are. The best ones pinpoint your location to within half an inch—but these cost thousands of dollars!

Pack well

Take useful equipment such as a map, compass, water, emergency food, spare clothes, first aid kit, and a flashlight. But don't carry too much or your pack will weigh you down!

Be prepared

Learn useful skills such as first aid and how to **navigate** with a map and compass. Check weather reports and find out what the main hazards are on the route you'll follow, for example a river that could flood.

The red compass arrow always points north. Turn the dial so that "N" for north lines up with it.

EMERGENCY!

Even the best-planned trip can go wrong.
A sudden blizzard, avalanche, or rock slide
can lead to injury or leave you hopelessly lost.
So what should you do when disaster strikes?

Snowstorms can be sudden and heavy, making it almost impossible to see ahead. Make sure everyone stays together.

Don't panic

Try to keep a clear head.
Think before you act and
don't make a bad situation
worse. If you're lost, keep
calm and try to work out
where you are by looking
at a map or studying the
land around you. Could
you retrace your steps?

THRILL SEEKER

Scott Mason (U.S.)

FEAT
Survived 3 nights on a mountain
by making an emergency shelter

WHERE AND WHEN
Mount Washington,
2009

Find shelter

If you're injured, unwell, or in danger, try to reach somewhere safe and sheltered, such as a cave or steep bank. Use rocks, branches, or snow to make a **lean-to** or other shelter, with any spare waterproofs or a **tarpaulin** as a roof.

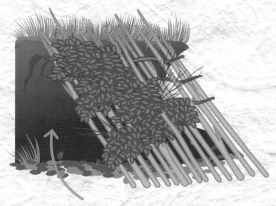

Long sticks covered with leafy branches (above) make a good forest shelter, while a tarpaulin (left) shades you from hot desert sun.

Call for help

If you're stuck in the mountains, the standard distress call is six whistle blasts or six light flashes if it's dark. Wait a minute then start again. Rescuers will give three blasts or flashes in reply.

EXTREME BUT TRUE You can only survive three or four days without water. If stranded, look for sources of clear, flowing water, and boil it before you drink it.

GLOSSARY

carabiner

abyss
A very deep crack or valley.

adrenaline
A chemical that your body produces when you feel stress. It helps you spring into action!

anchor
A metal loop, bolt, spike, or other object that is drilled or wedged into rock or ice and used to fix rope in place.

avalanche
A large slide of snow, ice, or rock down a mountain.

carabiner
An oval metal ring used to join two things together, such as a rope and harness.

climbing chalk
Chalk that climbers put on their hands to keep them dry and soak up sweat, so they can grip better.

erosion
The gradual removal of rock and soil by wind, rain, and other weather conditions.

GPS receiver
A device that picks up signals from satellites in space and uses them to calculate its exact position on the Earth's surface. GPS stands for Global Positioning System.

lean-to
A simple shelter made of branches propped against something solid.

navigate
To find your way using a map, compass, and the natural features around you.

anchor

snow blindness
A painful eye condition caused by not protecting eyes from intense sunlight in snowy places. It makes eyes sore, red, and full of tears.

tarpaulin
A heavy, waterproof sheet, often made of thick cloth called canvas.

summit

summit
The highest point of a mountain.

WEBSITES

www.climbing.com
Discover all kinds of climbing tips, facts, photos, and videos.

www.active.com/outdoors/articles/beginner-s-guide-to-rock-climbing
Get started with rock climbing using clear, step-by-step guides for beginners.

www.usaclimbing.net
Read the latest climbing news and find out about events all over the U.S.

INDEX

adrenaline 11, 22
anchors 9, 12, 22
avalanches 9, 20, 22

backpacks 7, 15, 19
balance 9, 10, 17
belaying 8, 12, 13
blizzards 14, 20
boots 7, 15

carabiners 12, 22
climbing chalk 7, 22
climbing walls 11
clothing 7, 14, 15, 19
compasses 7, 19
crampons 15

first aid kits 19
flashlights 19, 21
footholds 4, 7, 10, 11, 15
frostbite 15

GPS receivers 19, 22

handholds 10, 15
harnesses 6, 7, 9, 12
helmets 6

ice 7, 14, 15, 16
ice axes 15

knots 9

maps 7, 19, 20
Matterhorn 11
Mount Everest 4

navigating 19, 22

rock hopping 17
rock shoes 7
ropes 6, 8, 9, 12, 13, 16

scrambling 16, 17
shelters 15, 20, 21
slacklining 9
snow 7, 9, 14, 15, 20, 21
snow blindness 7, 23
snowstorms 20
sunglasses 7

tarpaulins 21, 23
training 5, 10, 11